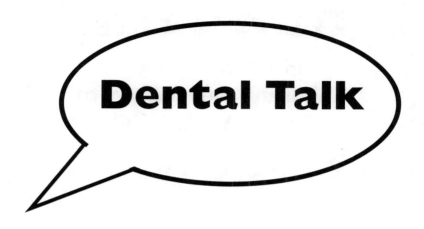

How to Manage Children's Behavior with Effective Verbal Skills

Thomas Haller
Chick Moorman

Personal Power Press
Merrill, MI

Dental Talk

How to Manage Children's Behavior with Effective Verbal Skills

© 2005 Thomas Haller, Chick Moorman, and
Personal Power Press

Library of Congress Catalogue Card Number
2005906559

ISBN 0-9616046-9-7

Printed in the United States of America

Personal Power Press
P.O. Box 547
Merrill, MI 48637

Cover Design
George Foster
www.fostercovers.com

TABLE OF CONTENTS

INTRODUCTION

There is a simple theme running throughout this book. It is that your choice of words, your style of communication, and the way you talk to children profoundly affect their attitudes, behavioral responses, and reactions to the dental experience. How you communicate with your young patients influences their actions as well as the outcomes that follow. By carefully choosing your words and style of speaking, you can help children become more relaxed, cooperative, and supportive of the job you need to do. That's what *Dental Talk*, the skills-based system described in this book, is about. It will teach you a series of verbal skills and language patterns that will reduce your stress, cut down on negative behaviors from your young patients, and enable you to accomplish what needs to be done with a minimum of hassles, frustrations, and power struggles.

Dental practitioners frequently find themselves struggling to manage a child's behavior as they attempt to provide needed dental care. A recent survey we conducted that included dental practitioners from over two hundred offices throughout the United States revealed that a large number of children enter the dental office already in a state of fear and locked into a mode of noncompliance. As a result, a declining number of dental practitioners are willing to work with children.

Children who are difficult to work with are often referred to a specialist. In many states, pedodontists report being overwhelmed with the number of difficult cases they are being asked to handle.

Working with children who are cooperative is not easy for the pedodonist or the family dental practitioner. The uncooperative child provides an even bigger challenge. Both categories of young patients require adults who have the knowledge, the skills, and the motivation to achieve the goal of providing quality dental work in a humane way.

While conducting research for this book we personally visited a variety of dental offices. We saw and heard stories of children who run out the door, refuse to open their mouths, bite, kick, scratch, swear, scream, and throw tantrums.

We also found some ineffective behavior on the part of the professional staffs. Unskilled practitioners often said or did things that fueled the misbehavior of children and in some cases instigated it. Children were expected to not fidget, wiggle, explore, ask questions, gag, grab, or struggle. In essence, they were expected to act like miniature adults. In some instances, any fear that the children had upon entering the dental office was exacerbated by the way they were talked to, treated, and physically handled. Several pedodontists suggested in our survey that the way the family dental practitioner handled children initially was a contributing factor in the referral to their office.

Power struggles were common. Some struggles occurred because the family dental practitioner moved too fast. Some were a result of misconceptions the child developed before he or she arrived. Others were due to the dental team handling children in a way that met the needs of the staff while being oblivious to or ignoring the needs of the child. One pattern that quickly emerged in our research is that once a problem developed a referral to a pedodontist quickly followed.

The pediatric dental offices we visited handled noncompliant children in a wide variety of ways. In some offices, the children were physically carried to a room called an 'operatory' and strapped to a papoose board while the necessary procedure was performed. In these offices the parents were instructed to remain in the waiting room while the frightened and sometimes screaming child was taken down the hall, where dental personnel did their work.

Other offices reflected a calmer environment. The rooms were colorful and child friendly. The dental practitioners talked to children in soft gentle tones, explaining every procedure and tool and using silly and weird names for the dental equipment. Parents were included in much of the process and were given specific directions by the dental practitioner. Sometimes they were told exactly what to do, where to stand, and when to speak.

No one would disagree that there are times when dental procedures need to be performed on children. Some are routine, some are emergencies, some are extraordinary, but at some point in a child's life dental treatment will become necessary. Just as they need routine medical procedures that may hurt, children need to go to the dentist, even though there may be some temporary pain or discomfort involved.

Your job would be a lot easier if children understood the importance of health- related procedures that are necessary for their well-being. But most of them are not old enough, mature enough, or experienced enough to understand and appreciate your efforts.

Whatever your role in the dental office, you know that children are going to be anxious, frightened, sometimes terrified. At times they will experience discomfort and pain. Yet, you have a job to do. You have a tooth to fill, x-rays to take, surgery to perform, or teeth to turn pearly white. You have to numb, drill, scrape, extract, or install braces.

While what you do is important, so too is how you choose to BE when you do whatever it is that you do. What kind of dental practitioner do you want to be with children? Do you want to be time-efficient, controlling, friendly, patient, abrupt, nurturing, affirming, educational, authoritarian, kind, calm, confrontational, flexible, challenging, empowering, judging, accepting, stoic, or argumentative?

Take a moment and think about your commitment to dentistry. What is your highest vision of yourself as the best dentist, pedodontist, dental assistant, or dental hygienist you can possibly be? Does your personal vision include relationship building along with task completion? Do you see yourself as someone who is as concerned about your young patients' emotional state as you are about their physical state? Is building an environment of safety and trust as important to you as an office with state-of-the-art equipment? Is attending to children's spirits as much a priority for you as fixing their teeth? Is who you are as a human being of equal value with who you are as a dental practitioner?

If your highest vision of yourself as a dental practitioner includes trust, caring, empathy, relationship building, and attending to a child's spirit as you work on his or her teeth this book is for you. You will find that your choice of words and your style of communication are crucial to achieving your highest vision. There is an undeniable link between the words you speak and the attitudes and outcomes of the children who enter into your care. By intentionally selecting words and phrases that foster feelings of security, build a sense of trust, and encourage self-responsibility, you can empower children and enhance their effectiveness in managing their own behavior, even in the stressful situation of visiting the dentist's office.

The book you hold in your hands offers a variety of verbal skills and language patterns that can strengthen your relationship with your young patients. It gives you verbal tools that you can put to use immediately to enhance your relationship with children and influence their behavior in a positive manner.

While *Dental Talk* is not intended to be a cure-all for your most difficult cases, it will definitely help you manage those situations with communications skills that reduce their severity while maintaining the dignity of everyone involved. The verbal skills presented here will help you create a preventive atmosphere where severe cases are less likely to occur.

In this book you will find signature phrases and language strategies that have a proven track record in creating a culture of trust, accountability, and cooperative behavior in schools, homes, and childcare facilities around the world. By improving communication and the relationship between you and the children you serve, you will foster an environment where they become less resistant and more willing to cooperate. By carefully choosing words and phrases that communicate respect and caring, you can set limits and shape desired behavior without wounding the spirit of the children you work with.

The phrases and supporting rationale in *Dental Talk* are designed to help you take an in-depth look at how you talk to the children you serve in your dental practice. The intent is to provide you with new perspectives on old patterns of communication, along with an array of possible new choices.

Use *Dental Talk* to become conscious of your language patterns and the effects that your style of speaking has on children and parents. Use it as a resource to strengthen how you communicate with the young patients who enter into your care. Use it to improve your skills and learn to do even better what you already do well.

You decide which phrases will enhance your skills as a dental practitioner and create the outcomes you want with the children you serve. Select those that support your own attitudes, philosophy, and beliefs as a dental practitioner. Choose and implement the concepts that appeal to you.

We recommend that as a group your office staff pick two or three phrases that address the behaviors you see frequently in your practice. Put them on file cards and display them in places where the staff will notice them often. Use the cards as a reminder to each other to use the selected phrases. Work together toward making the phrases a regular part of your communication style with children. As a phrase becomes a regular part of your staff's language patterns, add another phrase or two. Over time you will change the language patterns of those in the entire dental office to produce the results you want as a dental practitioner.

We encourage you to visit **www.dentaltalk.net** and sign up immediately for our FREE e-zine for parents. Make copies of the e-zine to give to your adult patients who are parents. When parents learn and use the same verbal skills they hear you using, their children's response to you will be faster and smoother.

While visiting us at **www.dentaltalk.net** be sure to order the brochure, *"Your Child and the Dentist: How* *to Give Your Child A Successful Dental Experience."* Mail the special report to every new client prior to their first visit to your office. When parents and practitioners follow these guidelines, you will be amazed at the child's positive response to you during that all-important first visit.

Working with children is a never-ending challenge. To those of you who choose to do it, we salute you. May this book lighten your load and make the difficult job of working with anxious, fearful children easier on them, their parents, and especially you, the enlightened dental practitioner.

Chapter 1

CONNECTEDNESS

"MY BABY TEETH ARE NOT DECIDUOUS!
I BRUSHED THEM!"

"Welcome, Bill. It's good to have you here."

You never have a second chance to make a first impression. And the person who makes the first verbal contact, the first human impression, in your dental office is the receptionist.

Teach your staff to welcome new clients verbally, particularly the children. Would it surprise you to know that many receptionists speak to the parent who enters the office and virtually ignore the child? Verbally recognizing the child using his or her name is essential to creating an inviting atmosphere. A big smile added to the greeting is helpful. Asking questions about age, interests, or how many previous visits the child has had to the dentist continues the acclimation process as he slowly gets used to the unfamiliar environment.

The appearance of your office, the sounds, and the visual stimuli that greet your young patient send a message that he is taking in and using to form opinions. All this happens before he even sees you for the first time.

Having your staff arrange appointments so that children don't sit in the waiting area too long helps reduce anxiety about what is to happen. If children are sitting around with nothing to do, apprehension builds. Providing materials of interest for different age levels will help as well.

A skilled receptionist can monitor the waiting environment and intervene if necessary. Taking an interest in the child by asking what he is reading, pointing out the fish tank, or suggesting age-appropriate toys helps build rapport with the dental staff and dissipates mounting anxiety.

"Welcome,
Michael.
My name is..."

The sweetest sound in any language is the sound of our own name. Names get our attention, build connectedness, and help us to bond. Begin immediately by introducing yourself, using your young patient's name. Ask him what name he would like to be called. Many children prefer a variation of the name printed on their chart. Then use his name regularly throughout the course of the session.

Using the child's name and letting him know what name he can call you may seem incidental. It is not. It is crucial in the process of managing a child's behavior.

When you introduce yourself in this way, several things occur simultaneously. First, by saying the child's name you draw her attention to you and she begins to believe that you know her and are her friend. Children unconsciously think, If you know my name, then you must know me. You have a better chance of getting the child to follow your directions if she believes that you are connected to her.

Be sure to say the child's name not just when you introduce yourself. Use it throughout the time he or she is with you.

Use it at the beginning of a sentence.

> *"**Mary**, will you turn your head toward me a little more, please?"*

> *"**Anthony**, hold this tight between your teeth."*

Use it in the middle of a sentence.

> *"Hold real still, **Emily**, while I take a picture of your teeth."*

> *"Follow me, **Pedro**, and I'll show you the fancy chair you get to sit in."*

Use it at the end of a sentence.

> *"I like the way you did that, **Julie**."*

> *"I need you to hold as still as you ever have, **J.D.**"*

We encourage you to use the child's name frequently to position yourself as a friend, a confidant, and a helper. Let go of the need to position yourself as the authority or the one in charge. Children already know that you're the boss, and they feel tension because of it. Building connectedness is far more important than establishing the hierarchy of power and control.

Second, get down on the child's level when you talk to him. Bend down so that you can look into his eyes. Children spend much of their lives looking up at adults who are talking down to them. By bending down you demonstrate that you respect them and are willing to do what it takes to care for them. Being seen as a caregiver is far more beneficial than being seen as an authority.

Children feel honored and empowered when you use their names and talk to them on their level. Youngsters who feel empowered without our having to use manipulation to get that power are more likely to follow directions and manage their own behavior in appropriate ways.

Third, when you use a child's name it shows interest, communicates caring, and extends feelings of compassion. The survey we conducted with dental practitioners from around the country indicated that children's fear is a major contributing factor to unmanageable and disruptive behavior in the dental office. When children hear their names said with warmth and kindness, a measure of comfort settles into their body, reducing their internal fear and anxiety. Any step you can take in reducing a child's fear will move you closer to accomplishing the goals you have for his or her visit to your office.

"IT'S A PARTNERSHIP, EDDIE, NOT A DENTIST GLUT."

"*I noticed...*" is Dental Talk that communicates to the child, I see you. You are important here. You are visible to me. I notice you. Everyone likes to be noticed. Being noticed builds self-esteem and communicates to the child that he or she is valuable and appreciated.

Use "*I noticed...*" statements in two different ways. First, point out or "notice" specific things about the child with whom you're working.

"***I noticed*** *you like to wear red.*"

"***I noticed*** *you brought a teddy bear friend with you today.*"

"***I noticed*** *you have a bow in your hair.*"

By using "noticing" language, you build a rapport and a level of trust with the child directly. The more of a relationship you can build with him or her, the more leverage you have in the behavior management process. A child's motivation to behave does not come from fear of punishment but from being in a relationship.

We teach this key concept to educators in our classroom management seminars. We encourage educators to focus their effort in the first three or four weeks of school on connecting each day with every child one-on-one and learning about the child's likes, dislikes, favorite color, and other personal information. At the same time, the teacher is to give personal information to the child that connects the two of them in some way. Those teachers who concentrate on this concept have more success when they implement classroom management later in the school year.

While we realize that you don't have this kind of time, you do have the child's chart, where some of this information can be gathered beforehand in a brief questionnaire sent home to parents when they schedule the first appointment. Or it can be filled out in the waiting room at the first visit (to assure that you actually get the questionnaire back). The parent can fill out part of the questionnaire with the child. Many offices have a health history form that the parents complete at the first visit. Additional questions designed to gather personal information can be added, such as, What's your favorite food? What's a favorite game you like to play? What's your favorite movie? Where do you go to school?

When you meet the child, you can use the questionnaire to engage her in conversation. "*I noticed* on the questionnaire that you like Star Wars movies." You can then establish commonality by referring to your own likes. "My favorite Star Wars character is Yoda. What's yours?" With just a few questions, in less than a minute you can build a relationship with the child that brings you one step closer to getting compliance.

Second, you can use *"I noticed..."* statements to draw attention to a desired behavior as it occurs. The goal is to reinforce the behavior so the child will continue to replicate it.

Children aren't always aware of their behavior, and an *"I noticed..."* statement can help them create a picture in their minds of themselves and the behavior they're exhibiting.

When you use the *"I noticed..."* phrase, descriptions are preferable to evaluations. The idea is to use a style of language that communicates to the child that you notice her, not that you evaluate, rate, or judge her. Refrain from language that gives an appraisal of her effort or behavior. Instead, notice the effort or behavior with a descriptive statement.

Examples of evaluative *"I noticed..."* statements:

*"**I noticed** you did a good job sitting still."*

*"**I noticed** you were wonderful at letting me take a picture of your teeth."*

*"**I saw you** being a good patient today."*

Examples of descriptive *"I noticed..."* statements:

*"**I noticed** you sitting still."*

*"I **noticed** you had your mouth wide open so I could see all your teeth."*

*"I **noticed** you holding your body still while I touched your teeth with this special instrument."*

Add *"I noticed..."* to your language with children. This signature phrase will help you develop a rapport and build trust between you and your young patients. It will also assist you in reinforcing a desired behavior and help them see themselves as capable and under control while at the dental office. In addition, use *"I noticed..."* with your colleagues. Say to them, *"I noticed* you've been implementing the Dental Talk phrases on a consistent basis," or *"I noticed* the positive effects your style of speaking is having on our young patients." Notice your own implementation efforts, and comment to yourself, *I noticed* how my language patterns with children have enhanced my effectiveness as a dental practitioner.

"I'm going to bend down so I can hear you better."

With this one phrase and the accompanying action of bending down you present several important concepts to the children who come into your care. First, by bending down so that you're on eye level with them, you change how they feel toward you. Children spend a large portion of their early years looking up at the world around them. Their world is large, confusing, and literally out of reach. When you physically lower yourself to their level, you open yourself up to them. They gain more access to you and begin to see you as approachable. The more approachable you seem to them, the more connected they feel to you. The more connected they feel, the more willing they will be to do what you ask of them later.

Second, by positioning yourself with your body and your words as an adult who is willing to hear and accept what the child has to offer, you encourage his thinking. Children are great thinkers, especially if we encourage that process. They see the world from a different point of view than we do. Their ideas are just as important to them as our ideas are to us. Allowing them the opportunity to share their ideas and encouraging them to do so empowers them and provides a sense of control. When children are allowed to think and express their thoughts, they feel empowered. Empowered children are less likely to seek power and control through disruptive behavior.

Third, by adding, *"so I can hear you better,"* you indicate to the child that his words are important to you. You're saying that you value his opinion. The belief that "my opinion counts" is a vital component in building self-esteem and self-confidence. By seeking children's opinions and taking those opinions seriously, dental practitioners help their young patients expand their view of themselves as capable, responsible, valuable human beings. The result is children who are more willing to listen to your suggestions.

Fourth, by using your Dental Talk and your actions to get on the child's level, you encourage him to speak up. This can be invaluable to you, as children who speak up often provide you with important information you can use to figure out what is bothering them or to find an appropriate solution to a behavioral problem.

If a behavioral problem were to arise, you can ask these children for possible solutions. You can include their input as you attempt to reach consensus on a workable solution. There is always more than one way to solve a problem. A child's solution may be the one that works best for him. By taking children's suggestions seriously, you encourage their thinking, help them see themselves as problem solvers, and increase the chance that they will offer solutions in the future.

Go ahead, get eye to eye with your young patients. Let them know you're listening. The beneficial results are unending.

Chapter 2

INSTRUCTION

"I KNEW I'D RUB HOLES IN THEM WITH ALL THAT BRUSHING."

"**Let's practice.**"

If you want a behavior, you have to teach a behavior. Dental practitioners often ask children to behave in ways they have not been taught. You can save yourself a lot of time in the long run if you invest the time to teach specific behaviors up front.

"One of the things you'll be asked to do here is open your mouth real wide," Dr. Jenkins explained to a youngster on his first visit. "*Let's practice* a few times so you can learn to get good at it. This is just practice now. I'm not going to use my mirror or any of my other instruments until later. I just want you to practice. Open wide. Close. Open wide. Close again. This time open only a little bit. Now close. Open wide again. Close. I think you have it. Want to practice one more time before we do it for real? OK, open wide. Wow! That's the widest one yet. When you open that wide it really helps me do my job. Thank you. I believe you're ready for the real thing."

In addition to teaching the desired behavior, practice sessions give you the opportunity to provide corrective feedback if necessary or offer descriptive and appreciative praise. Practicing first helps the child get off to a positive start, experience success, and feel confident.

Children can practice putting the chair up and down, sitting still, or holding the x-ray material between their teeth. They can practice looking at your teeth, keeping their tongue off to the side, and keeping their hands out of your way.

You can even practice using the special strap that holds their head still while you perform delicate maneuvers that require complete stillness. When you practice something as important as using the head strap, you remove some of the fear and uncertainty. The child begins to relax as he gets used to the unfamiliar device. Trust grows as the practice sessions create confidence and familiarity.

You may be a dental professional who believes practice takes too much time. It does take time to practice opening wide, using the head strap, and other essential behaviors. However, investing that time on the front end will pay dividends later on. You will experience less frustration, get more cooperation, and have a smoother session if you allow your young patients to get comfortable with what you expect of them through practice.

If you're uncertain or unskilled at giving your young patients practice sessions, don't worry. You'll get better with practice.

*"**Next time,** please keep your hand down by your side."*

*"**Next time,** it would be helpful if you would keep your tongue on the other side of your mouth."*

*"**Next time,** hold up one finger if you want me to stop."*

"Next time" is a piece of Dental Talk that will help you plant positive pictures in the child's head of what you want to have happen in the future. The words you use following this sentence starter focus her attention on what you expect and encourage her to picture the positive behavior you want from her rather than the negative behavior you wish to eliminate.

Adding *"Next time"* to your Dental Talk does not guarantee the child will choose the desired behavior next time, but it will increase your odds that the appropriate behavior will occur.

"Next time, return the magazines to the magazine rack" is more positive than "Don't leave the magazines scattered all over."

"Next time, please go to the bathroom before I get you all set in the chair" is friendlier than "Don't come in here without going to the bathroom."

"Next time, put your gum in the basket on the way in" plants a more positive picture than "Don't come in here with gum in your mouth."

"Next time" concentrates on teaching. The words you use to follow *"Next time"* instruct. By describing the desired behavior, you give children useful information they can put to use in the future.

"Next time, use your indoor voice in the waiting room" teaches by making your expectation clear.

"Next time, wear your teeth guard when you do Tai Kwon Do" is instructive and communicates the behavior you want.

Are you interested in developing a style of communication that gives clear instructions about your expectations regarding your dental practice? Do you want children to create positive pictures in their heads of desired behaviors? Then, next time strengthen your Dental Talk with the sentence starter, *"Next time..."*

"Trying to talk when my hand is in your mouth doesn't work."

"Humming distracts me from the work I'm trying to do."

"Jerking your foot like that moves your whole body"

Commenting on the behaviors you want to eliminate has the opposite effect. It often increases the undesired behavior. When you give the child's negative behavior your attention, you inadvertently reward him by giving him what he wants. He successfully got you to stop the procedure in order to deal with his behavior.

Some behaviors are better off ignored altogether. If the behavior is not too distracting, you're better served by finding something positive the child is doing and mentioning that.

If you feel a strong need to say something, use Dental Talk to teach what needs to be done rather than focusing on what needs to be eliminated. *"Holding your foot still would be a big help to me"* is more instructive than "Jerking your foot like that moves your whole body." *"Please wait until I take my hand out of your mouth before you start talking"* plants a picture in the child's mind of the desired behavior. *"I need you to be totally quiet now so I can concentrate"* is more helpful than "Humming distracts me from the work I'm trying to do."

Ignore the negative behavior if you can. If you need to speak up, stay positive.

**"LOTS OF CANDY.
IT'S A GOOD THING CHICKENS DON'T
HAVE TEETH TO WORRY ABOUT."**

"I'll be putting this mirror in your mouth **because** I want to count your teeth."

"This is a strap that holds your head still **because** it's dangerous if you move it during this procedure."

"Please hold your arms down **because** your hand could bump my elbow and my special tool could touch the wrong tooth."

"Open your mouth wide so I can fit the tool in to see all of your teeth."

"Hold very still **because** I'm going to gently touch the sore tooth with my tool."

"I need you to keep biting down for one more minute **because** the impression is almost set."

One cause of dental anxiety in children is fear of the unknown. Explaining why you need to perform a procedure gives youngsters information. Information reduces the extent of the unknown. When the magnitude of the unknown is reduced, so is the anxiety level.

Children also manifest anxiety when they feel out of control. Repetitious orders without explanation contribute to that sense of helplessness.

Consider the stream of commands we heard delivered to a nine-year-old boy during a recent observation in a general practitioner's examination room.

"Sit still now."

"Open wide."

"Turn your head this way."

"More."

"Hold it."

"Stay right there."

"Don't move."

"OK, relax."

"Open again."

"Wider."

"Get your tongue out of the way."

"Keep your arm down."

"Turn more toward me."

A ten-minute deluge of commands was delivered without one explanation.

No one likes to be ordered around. We don't. You don't. And children don't. If you want to increase anxiety, resistance, and reluctance in your young patients, issue a barrage of orders devoid of explanation.

Children are more likely to comply with a request if there is a *"because"* attached to it. Why? Because they feel more in control and know more about why you're asking for a particular behavior.

Look carefully at the word "because." It's comprised of two words: "be" and "cause." When you give explanations, children are more likely to see themselves as cause. They get to *be* the *cause* of the requested behavior. Because they're going along with it and feeling in control, they're less likely to activate resistant and reluctant behaviors.

To help children be cause in your dental room, add the word because to your Dental Talk, accompanied by explanations.

Praise is the number one behavior modification tool used by both parents and teachers. It's not surprising, then, that the tool is often used by dental practitioners. Typical phrases include:

"You're being a good girl today."

"That is excellent behavior."

"You're showing an outstanding attitude."

"Superb effort on your part."

The name we give to this kind of praise is *evaluative*. It evaluates the child, her effort, her energy, or her attitude. While somewhat successful in getting children to behave, it is global in nature and rarely gives children direct information on the specifics of their behavior. In addition, it lacks two essential ingredients that could make it more effective.

To strengthen your verbal praise efforts, add descriptive and appreciative praise to the mix.

Descriptive praise describes accomplishments or situations and affirms rather than evaluates a behavior. *"You kept your mouth open for four minutes"* describes the situation. So does *"You kept your hands down and out of my way."* Descriptive praise does the teaching. It lets the child know what specific behavior was good. This is critical to effective praise because it helps the child internalize what good behavior in the dentist's office actually is.

Appreciative praise appreciates. It thanks the child and tells her the effect her behavior had on you or your office. *"Thank you for reading quietly in the waiting area. That helps my staff to get their work done"* is one example. Another is *"I appreciate it that you kept the noise down. That helps my other patients stay relaxed."*

Both descriptive and appreciative praise steer clear of evaluation. They leave room for the child to draw the conclusion, to make the evaluation. If you say, *"You went through the entire time using only one bib.* (descriptive) *That means I have many left for the other children. Thanks,"* (appreciative) the child can conclude, I did a good job. If your words are, *"You kept your hands out of your mouth the whole time.* (descriptive) *That really helps me do my job. Thank you,"* (appreciative) the child can say to herself, I was a good helper today.

Begin to strengthen the way you praise young patients. When you hear yourself saying, "Good job," stop and think. What was good about it? What specifically did the child do? How did it affect you or your office? Add descriptive and appreciative comments to your praise offerings.

As you begin to embellish your evaluations with descriptive and appreciative verbalizations, watch your young patients' eyes and faces. What you see there will convince you of the importance of this style of Dental Talk.

> ## "I like the way you're keeping your mouth open."

In most cases, you have less than an hour to get a child in the chair, explain the procedure, and complete it. That his behavior is cooperative and matches your expectation is critical to staying time efficient and productive.

Reinforcement theory offers important information to help you reach your goal of getting the job done in a timely manner while maintaining a positive relationship with the child. Simply stated, reinforcement theory reveals that the behaviors you reinforce with verbal and physical attention occur more often. The behaviors you ignore tend to extinguish themselves and occur less often.

A dental practitioner skilled in positive reinforcement using descriptive and appreciative praise can learn to shape children's behavior with gentleness and caring. Key components are learning to deliver the appropriate praise immediately after the behavior, offering it consistently throughout the session, and delivering it with a sincere tone.

The best time to praise a child is as soon as you see the desired behavior. As soon as his mouth becomes open enough for you to do your job effectively, deliver the praise, *"I like the way you're keeping your mouth wide open."* (descriptive praise) You can even add, *"That helps me do my job better."* (appreciative praise) Immediately upon entering the room after a successful x-ray episode, say, *"You held so still the pictures came out perfect. Now we can move ahead. Thanks."* This style of praise is much preferred to the global, non-specific praise of "You're being a good boy." Global praise does not help the child identify which behavior is helpful and is being appreciated.

Think of your verbal praise as a form of drip-feeding. One big "meal" at the beginning or end of the session is not going to create the behaviors you want. Young children need constant feedback in order to learn and perform the series of steps necessary to get them through the session successfully. If you wait until the end of the session to deliver praise you miss several opportunities to shape behavior during the session and you deny the child the opportunity to learn valuable lessons he could put to use next time. Learn to praise as you work... and often! "Drip" your descriptive and appreciative praise slowly over the course of the visit.

As you learn to use a positive reinforcement style of Dental Talk, do not overlook the importance of facial expressions, a light touch, and tone of voice. A smile or a pat on the shoulder along with your verbal praise will strengthen it and increase the chances that your positive reinforcement effort will hit the target.

Be sincere with your praise. Children are good crap detectors. They recognize phony praise that doesn't come from the heart. To make your praise sincere, focus less on using it to manipulate the child and more on giving him information about how he's doing and how it affects your efforts to complete the job.

**"THAT'S YOUR THIRD CANDY BAR.
BRUSH YOUR TEETH."**

"We give toys to all the kids who listen and behave."

"If you want a balloon, you'll have to sit still."

"You can have a coloring book if you do as I ask."

Bribing children with stickers, prizes, books, special privileges or any other external reward is ineffective. You do not help children learn to be cooperative with rewards. Rewards teach them that being cooperative in the dental chair is so difficult and so uncommon that rewards must be used to gain compliance.

One major problem with rewarding children is that it doesn't help them develop a commitment to cooperation or encourage them to keep choosing cooperation after the reward stops. When the payoff ends, so does the activity. At the end of the reward cycle children who are rewarded for doing an activity actually choose the activity less often than children who were never rewarded to begin with. In essence, your reward is creating children who will be less cooperative in the future.

When they are given stickers and trinkets, children don't come to see themselves as cooperative. They attribute their cooperative behavior to the reward, not to themselves or their attitude. They see themselves as a person who is cooperative for a sticker rather than as someone who is cooperative because it's helpful to you, helps get the job done faster, or is the right thing to do. They learn that the point of good behavior is getting a reward.

Rewarding children with stickers or providing any other form of external motivation actually harms internal motivation. As external motivation increases, internal motivation erodes. The more a child is rewarded externally for doing something like being cooperative in the dental chair, the greater the chance that he or she will lose interest in the activity once the reward ends. Then you have to move on to bigger and better rewards.

Stop the external reward cycle. Instead of a reward, give children real reasons why a specific behavior is important. Teach them that cooperation is important for the internal satisfaction it brings, the feelings of accomplishment that accompany it, and its helpfulness to others.

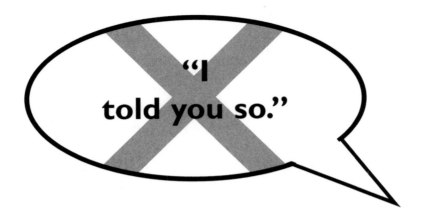

"See, I knew it. I told you that would happen if you didn't sit still."

"I guess that pain in your jaw proves I was right."

"That's what I said was going to happen if you didn't stop eating candy, remember?"

Being right feels good. It's a way of proving our worth to ourselves. There is only one problem. If you're interested in building a relationship with a patient, particularly with a young patient, being right doesn't work.

Being right breeds resentment. It activates resistance. Neither of those is what you want from someone who is leery of you to begin with. Any time you make yourself right, you make someone else wrong. Children do not relish being wrong. Saying, "I told you so," in any of its variations rubs the child's nose in the fact that he or she was incorrect. It's hard enough for children to accept being wrong without the additional pressure of having it brought to their attention.

Most of the time children realize they were wrong. They don't need to be told. An added reminder from you will only add to their mistrust and lessen the cooperation you need from the small human being sitting in the dental chair.

Refrain from using Dental Talk that proclaims your rightness. Gloat privately if you must. This is not the time to keep your mouth wide open. Keep it closed instead.

You've heard all the excuses.

"I couldn't find my retainer."

"My mother didn't buy any dental floss."

"I chew sugarless gum."

"I lost my toothbrush."

"I forgot."

"It's hard to remember over the summer."

When you hear one of the old standby excuses, or even a new one, it's probably tempting to respond, "That's not a good excuse." By giving children feedback on what we think of their excuses, we believe we're teaching them to behave more responsibly when it comes to dental care. Actually, this type of Dental Talk has the opposite effect.

When you say, "That's not a good excuse," you place yourself in the role of excuse judge. You communicate to the child that your role is one of excuse examiner and their role is to be the excuse giver. You imply with the words, "That's not a good excuse," that if they had a good one, you might accept it.

We suggest Dental Talk that keeps you from passing judgment on the excuse. Instead, use language that focuses on consequences and on the role children play in creating them. When a child says, "I couldn't find my retainer." reply, "I'm glad you found it and are using it now. I see that several of your teeth are beginning to get out of line already. If they get any worse, you'll be choosing to have braces again." Respond to "My mom didn't buy any toothpaste." with "Your mom's teeth don't look yellow. Yours do. It will take extra time today to get them clean."

Language that refuses to acknowledge excuses sends children helpful messages. They learn that your role is not that of judging excuses and that their behavior and the choices they make are more important to you than the excuse.

"Here
it is on paper."

Estimates suggest that over half of all information presented to patients is forgotten within the first five minutes of leaving the office. As time goes by, the percentage of information lost increases. And we're talking about adults here. Imagine what happens when the patient is an adolescent or a young adult.

Do you expect your teenage patients to remember what you told them about how to use their retainer? Do you think they will recall all the instructions you gave about after-surgery care? In most cases, it simply won't happen.

Your young patients are apprehensive about follow-up. They're concerned about how they will look and what their friends will say. Their current anxiety gets in the way and interferes with their ability to listen.

You can use the clearest Dental Talk in the world with these young patients, but if their listening apparatus is not functioning well, even the most succinct, clearly delivered message won't get through. If you have important information that the patient needs to retain, write it down.

Chapter 3

ANXIETY AND FEAR

"MY TOOTH DOESN'T HURT <u>THAT</u> BAD."

"Mom can stay here in the waiting room while we look at your teeth together."

Our survey of dental practitioners indicated that a major source of anxiety for children is parental involvement or the lack of it. When reviewing the comments made by these practitioners, we realized that there were actually two aspects to children's anxiety involving their parents: transfer anxiety and separation anxiety.

Dental practitioners observed that in many cases the parents transfer their own dental anxiety to the children. The parents exhibit so much anxiety themselves that the child can't help being anxious too. When anxious parents are in the exam room they often gasp, wince, and even groan as a procedure is about to begin. The practitioners also reported that anxious parents offer inappropriate reassurance with comments like "It won't hurt" or "Hold still for the shot." They inadvertently discuss negative aspects of the dental treatment within hearing range of their child. In a few reported cases, parents used the dental treatment as a threat, saying, "If you don't sit still and let the dentist fill that tooth he's going to have to pull it."

As a result, many practitioners have established firm views on whether parents should be present during dental treatment.

Thus, it may be necessary for parents to leave the exam area and allow the dental team to continue care in their absence. Many of the pedodontist offices we visited did not allow parents to leave the waiting room and enter the operatory area.

Regardless of when and where the separation takes place, many children experience separation anxiety. Simply being removed from the presence of a parent increases a child's anxiety and can result in disruptive behaviors such as crying and temper tantrums. However, the separation anxiety often occurs in the transition phase and subsides shortly thereafter. Kindergarten teachers and daycare providers are well aware that once the parent is out of the child's sight, the child shifts his focus to the person caring for him. Frequently within minutes the crying stops and the child redirects his focus.

While you're directing the Dental Talk phrase, *"Mom can stay here while we look at your teeth together,"* to the child, you might say to the parent in a gentle and calm manner, "The dental room is small. The waiting room is more comfortable." As you transition the child away from the parent to the examining room, redirect him with other Dental Talk phrases such as, *"I noticed..."* and *"Let me show you some fancy instruments."*

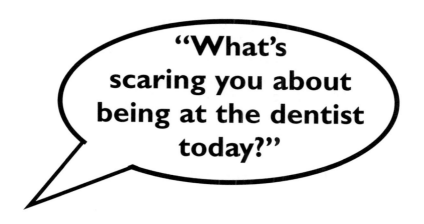

"What's scaring you about being at the dentist today?"

"What are you most nervous about right now?"

"You look scared. What has you most scared right now?"

"How come you're afraid?"

Yes, we are absolutely recommending that you ask children about their feelings. Many of the youngsters who come into your dental office are scared. They are afraid of something. It behooves you to find out what that is.

Our interviews with practitioners revealed a variety of answers from children who were asked this question.

"My mom said you're going to drill a hole in me."

"My brother said you're going to pull out all my teeth."

"Is it going to hurt?"

"What are you going to do to me?"

"I don't want you to cut all my hair off."

"I want my mommy."

"I'm afraid you're going to get my hair wet."

"My mom said you're going to put me to sleep. They buried Uncle Roger when he went to sleep."

"My sister said you stick needles in people."

"My friend said you have a thing that will suck my tongue out."

"I'm not supposed to talk to strangers."

As you can see, many of the children's fears were based on misconceptions and misinformation. By asking, *"What's scaring you about being at the dentist's today?"* you can find out what's behind the fear and begin providing children with accurate information.

Often, children begin to feel more comfortable just because you asked the question. This inquiry indicates that you have a genuine concern for them and their feelings.

When you find out what is scaring the child, address her concerns in a way that she can understand. Stay focused on providing information by telling her about the process and the steps you'll be taking to help her through it. Obviously, it's important to use age-appropriate language.

If a child is uncertain about why she's scared, let that be OK. Refrain from telling her why you think she might be frightened or why other children get scared at the dentist. There's a strong likelihood that she hasn't even thought about the things you will mention. By bringing them up you plant them in her consciousness and give her more issues to be scared about.

Instead, begin the process of reducing fear by informing the child about what she can expect to happen. Slowly and gently, keep her informed during each step in the process. Take your time and talk in a friendly manner. Keep your anxiety to a minimum and you'll help reduce hers.

"I'll do that last."

"When do I get the shot?" asked the nervous teen. "Not until I finish my exam and prepare the materials. It should be in about ten minutes," the dentist replied.

"I hate that gritty-tasting polish," the ten-year-old patient told the hygienist. "Does that happen pretty soon?" "Not for a long time," the hygienist replied. "I won't do that until the end. It comes last."

In each case, the child experienced an acute case of anxiety because he knew that something he found unpleasant would happen but he didn't know when. Just knowing when something will occur often helps children to relax and be less fearful. If nothing else, at least they know when to get anxious. In the meantime, they can be more relaxed until the time they fear actually arrives.

The unknown can create a deep level of concern for a child. Remove that concern by telling him when you intend to do specific procedures.

"KEEP YOUR EYES OPEN AND YOUR MOUTH SHUT."

> # "How can I help you feel more comfortable?"

"Are you OK?"

"How can I help you?"

"Do you feel all right?"

"Can I help you relax?"

This style of Dental Talk, using empathetic questions, communicates to children that you care about them and are concerned for their well-being.

So why should you care if children think you care about them? Simply put, studies have shown that the attitude of the dental practitioner toward the child patient is a significant factor in determining the child's behavior during the dental visit.

Children are notorious for patterning their responses in a situation to the responses of the adults around them. You've witnessed this phenomenon many times - for example, being confronted with an anxious child who is reacting to the nervous father who brought him in for his checkup. This behavioral patterning can also be triggered by the professionals in the dental office. Children's perception of the dental practitioner's level of care and concern has a large impact on their anxiety responses.

If you see children as a bother and as taking too much of your billable time, your young patients may be tuning into your subtle cues and picking up on your attitude toward them. If you attempt to hurry children through the process so you can get the job done quickly, they feel rushed and anxious. You don't have to tell them that you're in a hurry and that you resent having to be patient with them because it's costing you money. They pick it up from the vibrations you send out.

As a dental practitioner, you can use your attitude and behavior as a tool to manage children's behavior. Your attitude is important. The tone and volume of your voice are crucial. Just mouthing the right words is not enough. Simply using appropriate language without an accompanying attitude of caring and empathy will have little impact.

Demonstrate an attitude of caring to children through tone and volume, as well as through the language you use. Let your behaviors become congruent with your words and the youngsters will know that you care for them and are concerned about their feelings.

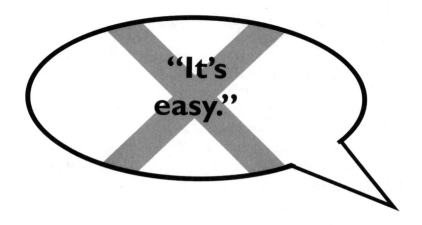

"It's easy."

Brenda sat rigidly in the dentist chair. Her small hands gripped her legs tightly. Signs of exasperation revealed her frustration with the necessity to hold still while the impression of her teeth was setting. Wanting to encourage the child and communicate his faith in her ability to persevere, the dentist told her, "Hang in there, Brenda. You can do it. It's easy." He didn't know that his well-intentioned words had trapped Brenda in a no-win situation.

The healthcare provider who encourages a young patient with, "it's easy," may inadvertently initiate feelings of anxiety and fear. Brenda was afraid of appearing incompetent. He says it's easy, she said to herself. What if I can't do it? I must really be bad.

On the other hand, Brenda might have used the dentist's comments to keep going. She might have breezed through the rest of the waiting period and discovered it was indeed easy for her. What amount of satisfaction could she then feel, knowing that what she accomplished was easy? She would likely only feel relief that she was able to do it without appearing incompetent. Her inner dialogue would be, "Of course I did it. Anybody could have done it. After all, it's easy."

A third possibility is that Brenda might have completed the task successfully but with great difficulty. Instead of feeling proud, she might then believe that a difficult task is beyond her ability because she had to struggle to complete something easy.

In each scenario Brenda can only lose by attempting a task the dental practitioner has pronounced as "easy."

We recommend you change your Dental Talk from "it's easy" to *"I think you're ready for this,"* or *"I know you can handle it."* "I think you're ready for this" does not address the difficulty of the task. That interpretation is left to the child. "I know you can handle it" does not say that you know she'll be able to do it. It states merely that you know she can *handle* it, which means that she'll either be able to do it or cope successfully with the consequences.

Your choice of language can communicate faith in your young patients' capabilities while simultaneously encouraging their efforts. And you can do that best if you eliminate "it's easy" from your language patterns. We know that you can handle this.

"Let me show you some fancy instruments."

"He sure was uncooperative," the dentist complained to the receptionist following the exit of a five-year-old first-timer. "Yeah, I knew five minutes after he came in it was going to be that way," the receptionist responded. The dental hygienist nodded in agreement. Consensus had been reached. The kid was uncooperative.

But was he really?

Children who are labeled "uncooperative" often get the label on their first visit to the dental office. In fact, the judgment often occurs within the first 20 minutes.

The behavior this judgment is based on is usually a reflection of how the child is feeling and his internal state. His response to you and the surrounding environment reflects a feeling of powerlessness. This child has limited communication skills. He doesn't understand what is going to happen to him. The objects around him are new and they look scary.

When children get scared, their fear triggers a fight-or-flight response. They try to cope by being disruptive in hopes it will allow them to escape. This doesn't mean they are uncooperative. It means they are five years old and scared.

You can gain the cooperation of a child by removing the fear of the unknown and sometimes by correcting inaccurate information and perceptions. When you do that, you put the child in the position of having power over his or her feelings.

Knowledge is power, even for children. Increase their knowledge base and reduce the unknown by explaining to them what is going to happen. It's important that you do this on a level they can understand. Tell them about the instruments. Explain their function. Allow your young patients the opportunity to touch, hold, and use some of the instruments. Let them play with the chair, look in the mirrors, put on rubber gloves, use the light to observe things.

Introduce the dental instruments and procedures gradually. Through a process known as acclimation, you take a child with no dental experience and help him become ready to receive dental care. A widely used technique for working with children with low to moderate anxiety is to begin by explaining the procedure, then demonstrating it either on a hand puppet or on the child's finger (e.g., a low-speed hand piece on the finger) and, lastly, initiating the procedure. Using this technique slowly moves the child into a receptive mode.

To assist in the acclimation, make the process fun and interesting. Give the instruments silly or weird names that children can relate to and identify with.

Some examples we heard while visiting dental offices were especially creative.

Low-speed hand piece	-	Mr. Bumpy
High-speed hand piece	-	Mr. Whistle
Nitrous mask	-	Mr. Elephant,
		Mr. Snoopy,
		The Astronaut
Air/water syringe	-	Water Squirter
High-volume suction	-	Mr. Thirsty,
		Vacuum Cleaner
Explorer	-	Tooth Counter

As an office staff, brainstorm names together and experiment with fun ways to present the instruments and the procedures to children. When you have fun with children, they loosen up and begin to have fun with you.

Remember, the goal is to instill a lifelong positive attitude toward visiting the dental office. That process begins with removing the fear of the unknown and empowering your young patients with knowledge.

"I DIDN'T KNOW UMPTEEN WAS A
REAL WORD."

"No pain is involved in this."

"I'm just going to drill this tooth for a moment."

"I use a needle to put it to sleep."

Dental practitioners who use sentences such as these do so with positive intentions. Their motto is, "No surprises." They believe that keeping children informed is the best policy for building a trusting relationship and gaining their cooperation. While we agree in principle, language such as that above may undermine their intent. Let's take a closer look.

The words you use with young children are important. Words plant images in their minds. These images create strong feelings and internal reactions.

For example, if we tell you, "Don't think of a blue elephant," what image comes to mind? That's right - a blue elephant. Even when we tell you not to think of a blue elephant, your brain focuses on the idea of a blue elephant and creates the image in your mind.

This principle holds true with the words you use to refer to the dental instruments or the procedures you are using. If you tell a youngster, "This isn't going to hurt," you plant an image of pain in her mind. If you say, "This is a sharp tool," you invite her to associate your instrument with other sharp objects she has experienced in the past. Many of those sharp instruments were dangerous. Some inflicted damage. If you say, "There is nothing to worry about," you plant the suggestion that there is, indeed, something to worry about.

It is imperative that you avoid using certain key words such as *sharp, hurt, needle,* and *drill.* These words are frequently associated with pain and discomfort and have the potential of increasing a child's anxiety.

We recommend that you give the child a positive picture of procedures and equipment with words and phrases that create images of comfort. Say, "It's relaxing to sit in this chair. It's built for comfort." It's fun to have your teeth polished." "Getting a picture of your teeth is cool. We can see them on fancy film."

Use descriptive Dental Talk to let the child know what will be happening and how you will be helping her to be comfortable.

"This comfortable chair helps me to see your teeth better."

"We have special medicine to rub on your tooth. It makes it go to sleep and feel tingly."

"This machine has a little camera in it that helps us see inside your teeth."

"We have a special way to make one tooth go to sleep and the rest stay awake."

"I have a tool that wipes the germs off your teeth."

"I can fill the holes that germs make in your teeth with special teeth putty."

Needle, syringe, and *drill* are words to avoid at all times. Also, keep these instruments out of children's view until the last possible moment. The sight of them too early creates unnecessary stress and anxiety.

When using needles, drills, and other scary equipment, use Dental Talk during the procedure that includes positive, descriptive language. This gives the child accurate information and plants a positive image about what is taking place. The more positive and upbeat the dental practitioner is during these times, the less anxious the child will be. Your choice of words can help you accomplish this goal.

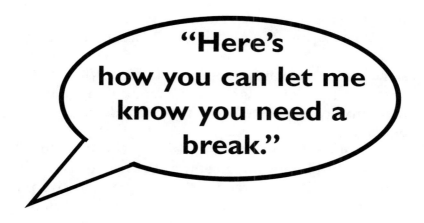

"Here's how you can let me know you need a break."

"Let's make a signal."

"This will stand for time out."

"When you need to say something, do this with your hand."

"Here's how you can let me know you need a break" and similar phrases create an atmosphere of shared control between the patient and the dentist. With shared control, the practitioner, who is very much in control, provides the child with an opportunity to have control of a small portion of the process.

"Here's how you can let me know" puts the child in control of announcing when he needs a break from sitting still, holding his mouth open, getting a shot, or having a tooth drilled. The dental practitioner remains in charge of the majority of the procedure and the child gets to feel like he has some control of the situa-

tion. Both are in control of a portion of the process.

When a shared-control phrase is accompanied by a stop signal such as raising a hand, it gives the child some say over what is happening to him. When children feel they have even a small amount of control, their anxiety is lessened. When anxiety decreases, so do the number of behavioral outbursts.

Another benefit of establishing a system that shares control with the patient is a perceived reduction in pain. Patients report that using a stop signal during routine dental treatments reduces feelings of discomfort and pain. Using this approach allows children to learn they have some control over their pain and anxiety.

Why not create a stop signal together with your young patients at the beginning of a session? Then review the signal on follow-up visits. Practice using the signal several times.

Realize that children may overuse the signal at first. They're testing the system to make sure it works and to see how much control they really do have. By responding every time to their request to stop you build trust in the system and trust in you. You further your efforts to build a relationship with the child that could extend over a lifetime.

"Let's
take a break."

Dr. Wilson noticed his patience running out with a teen who asked what seemed like an endless stream of questions. The tightening in his gut was his main clue.

Marjorie Hanniper, a dental assistant, observed and listened while the mother and the dentist tried to convince a preschooler to sit in the chair. When both adult voices began to get louder, she knew it was time.

Raymont Garcia heard what he interpreted as two rude remarks from his young patient. Then he heard sarcasm coming from his own lips. The sarcasm was his primary signal.

Dr. Wilson, Margarie Hanniper, and Raymont Garcia each recognized that it was time for a change of pace. Each employed an important Dental Talk phrase: *"Let's take a break"*

Use *"Let's take a break"* to keep a situation from escalating out of control. Use it if frustration is getting in the way of listening. Use it if your emotions are rising to a level that will affect your ability to do the work that needs to be done.

"Let's take a break" means exactly that. It's a time-out, taking a break from the heat of a struggle. It's an opportunity for everyone involved to regain composure, relax, and begin again.

Great basketball coaches know when to take a break. They know when to call a time-out. They do it when their team has lost its composure or focus. They do it if their players are not using the skills they learned in practice. They do it if they need a moment to think and revise the game plan.

Follow the lead of successful basketball coaches. Call a time-out if someone in your treatment room has lost his or her composure, deviated from the game plan, or needs to refocus. *"Let's take a break"* may be just the Dental Talk you need to get things back on track.

Chapter 4

FEELINGS

"NO, HE ISN'T GOING TO CLEAN AND SHARPEN THEM. HE'S JUST GOING TO CLEAN THEM."

"There's no reason to be afraid."

"You're overreacting. It's not that bad."

"I haven't given you anything to cry about."

"There's nothing to be scared about."

"You're being way too sensitive about this."

"It takes more muscles to frown than it does to smile."

These Dental Talk sentences are examples of trying to talk a child out of her feelings. They are all doomed to failure. Save your breath. They do not work.

Feelings are not rational. They do not need logical, reality-based reasons to give them validity. They just are. They are real for the child, and for that reason alone you're better served to treat them as real.

A child caught in strong emotion is not in a position to listen. This is not an appropriate time to lecture, reprimand, give advice, try to talk her out of her feelings, or distract her from what is going on inside.

In times of strong emotion, children need support. They need adults who will help them work through their feelings in safe ways. That includes you, the dental practitioner. What children need from you before they are emotionally ready to move on is an emotionally supportive environment where their feelings are acknowledged and validated. They need Dental Talk from the dentist, hygienist, assistant, and receptionist that is in direct opposition to the language above.

Your agenda of moving on with a relaxed and cooperative patient is better served by encouraging the child to feel and express her emotions. It is only after emotions are expressed that children are able to handle the problems and concerns that relate to those feelings. It is not until the negative feelings come out that there is room for positive feelings to emerge.

To help your emotion-charged young patient, use words that identify the feeling she's acting out. *"You sound frustrated"* and *"I hear how angry you are at me for poking around in your mouth"* acknowledge that you recognize the child's feelings. *"You seem irritated to have to be here"* and *"You really are annoyed with this whole process"* demonstrate that you're listening on a feeling level.

Using Dental Talk to cheer children up or talk them out of their feelings is ineffective. It tells them that feelings are not good, that their feelings are wrong, and that feelings will not be honored in the dental office. None of this is helpful if a long-term relationship with a cooperative client is your goal.

"Sounds like you're feeling frustrated."

Young children often reveal a limited vocabulary when they try to verbalize their feelings. Ask a youngster how he's feeling and you're likely to hear, "OK," "good," or "bad." This three-word preference for describing feelings can be attributed to two factors. First, children are not always in touch with their feelings. Second, even when they're aware of their feelings they don't have a variety of words in their vocabulary to describe those feelings accurately.

A Dental Talk strategy to help children recognize and express feelings appropriately is to act as a mirror and reflect their feelings back to them. The more they express their feelings verbally, the less they act them out in disruptive behaviors. Encourage your young patients to talk about how they're feeling and help them put words to what you observe in their behavior. When a child is expressing anger, you can mirror that expression by saying, *"I can see the aggravation on your face,"* or *"You look angry. Tell me about that."* When fear

74

appears to be the predominant feeling, you can say, *"You look scared. Is there anything you'd like to ask me?"* or *"You look pretty nervous right now. We'll go slowly and I'll explain everything to you as we go."*

Unless it has been modeled for them consistently, children won't often tell others how they're feeling. They may need the dental practitioner's help to recognize and articulate those feelings as well as to understand that communicating feelings is worthwhile.

Mirroring the feeling of your young patients can help them appreciate the value of sharing feelings and reduce the likelihood that they will act on those feelings in disruptive ways.

The 15 Worst Things to Say to Your Young Patients

"Why can't you be more like your sister?"

"Knock it off."

"If you don't brush, you'll lose all your teeth."

"You're acting like a baby."

"Big boys don't cry."

"That's disgusting."

"If you don't stop that I'm going to have to knock you out."

"I going to have to tell your mother how bad you are."

"Where are your manners?"

"Because I said so, that's why!"

"You ought to be ashamed of yourself."

"Don't do that."

"I tell you when you can take a break."

"You'll be fine. I promise."

"You won't feel a thing. Trust me."

For a detailed explanation of why these sentences appear on "The 15 Worst Things to Say to Your Young Patients' list, visit us at **www.dentaltalk.net.**

"I understand just how you feel."

"I'm scared," seven-year-old Blake told the dental hygienist. Attempting to be empathetic, the veteran hygienist replied to the frightened youngster, "I understand just how you feel."

"I understand just how you feel" is language adults often use to reassure children that they too have experienced fear, doubt, anger, or frustration. The positive intention is to communicate, I know what it's like for you. I've been there too. I understand.

Nobody can understand exactly how another person feels. No two people, their experiences, or their perceptions of those experiences are ever the same. We're all different and so is each of our experiences of life, including our experience of sitting in the dental chair or having a cavity filled for the first time.

When children are experiencing strong emotion because a stranger is poking them with a sharp instrument or approaching them with a scary-sounding drill, part of them believes that they're the only person in the world who has ever felt this way. They want to be taken seriously for the uniqueness of their experience.

On the other hand, children want to know that their feelings are normal. They want reassurance that they will not be overwhelmed by their feelings, that others have survived the same emotions.

We suggest you drop "I understand just how you feel" from your verbal responses. Instead of *telling* your young patient you understand, *demonstrate* that you understand with active listening.

If a youngster tells you, "I'm scared," paraphrase what you hear and see. Say, *"You're frightened because you've never done this before."* Make it a statement, not a question. If he says nothing but looks frightened, say, *"You look nervous and seem to be unsure about what's happening."* *"You look like you're wondering what might happen next"* is another way to reflect a puzzled look.

Paraphrasing is a verbal skill that does not presume you understand. It's a reflective response used to check out the accuracy of your understanding.

If your words accurately reflect the child's feelings, he'll feel acknowledged and understood. He is then likely to say more. In addition, he'll be more relaxed and cooperative as you move forward with the job you need to do.

If your initial paraphrase is inaccurate, the child can correct the misconception by restating or embellishing his original comments. Either way, you arrive at understanding, connection, and increased cooperation.

Reflective listening is an act of respect for the youngster who sits frightened in your chair. It tells him, I don't know exactly how you feel, but I'm ready to listen and I want to understand. I'm willing to check it out and see if I got it right. Your feelings are important and you're worth this time and energy.

With practice, your active listening skills will improve. You will notice how much your young patients appreciate your efforts and how they are comforted and relaxed when they believe you really do understand their feelings and concerns.

"Your legs are kicking and your arms are swinging about."

Most dental practitioners at one time or another find themselves handling a child who is yelling, screaming, hitting, kicking, or refusing to move. The child simply refuses to cooperate, and continuing treatment seems impossible. Reasoning with him or her appears to make matters worse.

It is at this point (if not sooner) that most general practitioners give up and send the child to a pedodontist. This is also the place in the process where many pedodontists strongly consider sedation or referring the child to a hospital setting.

However, before you instigate such a drastic move, consider a useful verbal skill that may help you get the child back under control. We call this Dental Talk skill "reflecting."

Reflecting is a technique that stimulates the area of the brain that is the output and control center for behavior. This area, called the frontal lobe, helps people create choices, choose among options, compare possible outcomes, and manage behavior. Be assured that when a young patient is throwing a tantrum in the dental office she is not using her frontal lobe. Until you can get the child back to the frontal lobe, no amount of reasoning, analyzing, problem solving, or reassuring will help.

When a child demonstrates physical behaviors such as hitting, kicking, biting, stomping feet, throwing objects, and swinging arms, he or she is in tantrum mode. Such behavior is more closely associated with the midbrain, not the cortex, where the frontal lobe is located. Yelling, screaming, crying, and other emotional behaviors are generated in the limbic brain, which assists in managing emotional content and is not typically a behavior management area.

As a healthcare professional, it's important that you recognize these behaviors and understand that the child is not in an appropriate space to engage in or accept verbal directions. Attempting to reason and provide instruction in the middle of a tantrum or during an emotional outburst will serve no useful purpose. Using verbal language like "Stop wiggling and sit still" or "Stop crying and open your mouth" or "Throwing a tantrum won't get you what you want" will not bring about the desired result.

Your role at this point is to help the child pass through the tantrum phase, out of fight-or-flight mode, and into a behavior management mode. To move a child into her frontal lobe and thus into a space conducive to receiving verbal instruction, calmly use words to paint a picture of the behavior or emotions that you observe.

When a child is having a tantrum, say, *"Your legs*

are kicking. Your arms are swinging around. Your teeth are clenched and your body is moving all over the place." Reflect back to the child the behavior you're observing without criticizing or shaming her in any way. If a child is yelling and crying, reflect the emotional content by saying, *"I hear fear in your voice. You seem scared. Your voice is loud and echoing through the building."* By using the reflecting technique, you help children identify and recognize their behavior and emotion. As they do this, they become aware of themselves, and the frontal lobe becomes activated.

Chapter 5

CHOICE THEORY

"YOU PICK RAISINS OUT OF COOKIES, BILLY. WHY DON'T YOU PICK ROCKS OUT OF MUDPIES?"

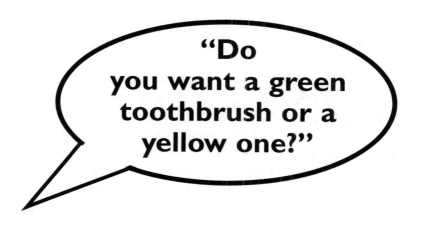

"Do you want a green toothbrush or a yellow one?"

Whenever feasible, give children choices. There is power in choice. By offering choices you empower the child and lessen the chance that he will decide to engage you in a power struggle.

"Would you like me to show you my tools first or take pictures of your teeth?"

"Would you like to hold the tissue or have your mom do it?"

"Shall I start on the top or the bottom?"

Use Dental Talk that offers controlled choice rather than unlimited choice. This is a shared-control style of child management in action. You have control because you control the number and type of choices. The child has control because he gets to pick from the choices offered. "You can have any toothbrush in the drawer" is an example of unlimited choice. "Red and yellow are the options today" reflects controlled choice.

Feelings of power and control are directly related to the number of decisions children get to make. Offering limited choices is a way of sharing control with them that often wins their cooperation and gives you more control in the end.

When a child gets to make no choices, he feels unempowered and out of control. In an effort to gain some control over his life he may choose resistance, reluctance, or defiance. Far better for you, the dental practitioner, to use Dental Talk that encourages children to exercise their power needs through the choices you offer them than to have them gaining power through resistance.

You can select Dental Talk that offers children choices or not. It's your choice.

"Please make a different choice."

The high-pitched, whining voice of the six-year-old in the waiting room carried into the office, beyond to the teeth-cleaning area, and beyond that to the two rooms where the dentist moved back and forth between patients. It could be heard all the way down the hall.

The boy's mother appeared unable or unwilling to manage the situation, and the distraction and annoyance of patients and the dental practitioners increased. The receptionist, closest to the source of the noise, had trouble hearing the telephone caller who needed to make an appointment. When she put the phone down at the end of her conversation, she decided to take action.

What would you do in this situation? Would you talk to the mother or the child? What would you say?

The receptionist had several choices. She could ignore the situation and hope it got better. She could tell the mother to please control her child. She could speak to the child and tell him to "knock it off."

The receptionist made a different choice. She walked toward the child, bent down until she was at his eye level, and said softly, "I'm being distracted by your behavior. It's difficult for me to do my job with this noise. *Please make a different choice."*

The receptionist did not scold, reprimand, or ridicule. She simply let the child know that his behavior was affecting her and suggested that he "make a different choice."

By telling the child to make a different choice, the receptionist used language that communicated respect. Her message informed him, I know you are responsible for your own behavior. I believe you are a bright boy. I know you can figure out what to do here.

She didn't tell him to "be quiet." She didn't threaten, "If you don't straighten up you'll have to leave." She didn't even tell him *what* to do. By suggesting that he make a different choice, she communicated that she trusted he was intelligent enough to choose an appropriate response. Her words told him emphatically that she felt he needed to choose differently, but she left the decision of what that choice was to him. Her communication let the child know that his actions affected her. That helped him understand that his actions have impact.

Use the phrase, *"Please make a different choice"* in your dental practice this week. When a child's behavior is interfering with your ability to work, tell him, "Your wiggling is getting in the way of my doing my job. *Please make a different choice."* "The goal is to keep your hands away from your mouth. *Please make a different choice."* "Books and magazines belong on the table or in the rack. *Please make a different choice."*

When children are disruptive or behave inappropriately, adults often attempt to change their behaviors by overpowering them with orders and commands. This tactic undermines the atmosphere of mutual respect and caring that is needed in a dental practitioner's office and is more likely to cause children to resist rather than change. *"Please make a different choice"* shares some power with them and acknowledges their responsibility for their own behavior. They are then more likely to respond appropriately by making a different choice.

"NOT <u>THAT</u> STIFF AN UPPER LIP."

"Act
as if..."

At the beginning of his first dental exam, eight-year-old Jason Miller was asked to hold still and open his mouth wide.

Brenda Hoskins, a middle-school student, was asked simply to turn her head more to the left.

Preschooler Carly Santana was informed she would be having a tooth put to sleep.

In each instance, the child replied, "I can't."

Whenever you hear "I can't" language in your dental office, be assured that it signals an "I can't" stance on the part of the child toward whatever you are attempting to accomplish. Often accompanied by a whiny tone, "I can't" words are connected to "I can't" thinking, "I can't" beliefs, and "I can't" behaviors.

How do you respond when one of your young patients looks up from the dentist chair and mumbles, "I can't do it"? What do you say? If you're like many of the dental practitioners we've observed and parents who attend our workshops, you reply with something like, "Sure you can. Come on, try." Perhaps you believe if they would just try, they'd be able to do it.

"Sure you can. Come on, try" sounds like helpful Dental Talk. It's not, because most often it doesn't work. Children typically respond with, "I'm trying," or "I tried already."

What many children and adults who work with them don't understand is that *trying* doesn't work. Only *doing* works. Anyone who is busy trying is not busy doing. *Trying* is often an excuse for giving up.

A strategic piece of Dental Talk to replace the "Come on, try" language is *"Act as if..."* The next time one of your young patients delivers a whiny rendition of "I can't," smile, look him in the eye and, with gentle authority, give him these three words, *"Act as if..."*

*"Billy, **act as if** you've done this before."*

"But I haven't done it before."

*"I know. That's why I want you to **act as if** you have."*

After you have delivered this piece of Dental Talk, it's your turn to "act as if." Act as if you expect the child to do it. Assume that he will follow through and watch what happens. We predict you will be pleasantly surprised by the results. This strategy will not work every time with every child, but it could well be an important addition to your verbal repertoire.

With very young patients, "Pretend like you can" or "Play like you've done this before" work well.

*"Tamika, **pretend** that you're good at this."*

"But I'm not good at it."

That's why I want you to **pretend.***"*

"Marinano, **play like** *you can do it."*

"I can't."

"I know. That's why I want you to **play like** *you're the best!"*

Sometimes children "act as if" and they begin doing the task incorrectly. Don't worry. You can correct incorrect doing. *Act as if, play like,* and *pretend* are designed to get kids moving, to get them off the "I can't" stance toward the dental experience. Once you get them moving, you can adjust. You now have a patient who is moving in the desired direction. Until they begin moving, corrective guidance is impossible.

Not sure "act as if" will work for you with your young patients? Not sure you can use this verbal tool effectively? Why not *act as if* you can?

"I want you to help me solve my problem."

Billy has trouble sitting still. Enrique displays passive-aggressive behaviors, sitting apathetically, barely going through the motions without full compliance with instructions. Joanna talks nonstop, making access to her mouth extremely difficult.

These children, from different parts of the country, different cultures, and different circumstances, have one thing in common. They are choosing a behavior that interferes with the dental practitioner's efforts to administer the necessary dental care. Each dental professional met the situation with the same verbal response: *"I want you to help me solve my problem."*

If wiggling in the chair bothers you, then it is *you* who has a problem. If apathetic compliance with your instructions is getting in the way of getting your job done, then *you* have a problem. If nonstop talking interferes with your work, once again it is *you* who has a problem.

Some health care professionals believe that in cases such as those cited above it's the child who has a problem. After all, they reason, the child is the one wiggling, talking, or displaying an apathetic attitude. The child is the one choosing the inappropriate and unhelpful behavior. The child is the one preventing dental work from being done efficiently and safely.

A different point of view, however, is that wiggling does not create a problem for the child. It is only irritable and frustrating to the dentist and the assistant. While it's true that both the young patient and the dentist will benefit from a change of behavior, it's really the *dentist* who has a problem.

If your verbal reaction to the problem comes across as if the child has a problem, the child will likely feel accused and wrong. The common reaction is resistance and defensiveness. When children feel pushed, they push back. The "you have a problem" stance fails to help you and the child move in the direction of generating a solution.

When adults communicate from the "I have a problem and I want your help" approach, children are more cooperative. They are more likely to understand your problem and less likely to view you as an adversary.

When you invite children to help you solve *your* problem, you encourage them to join you in the search for solutions. You ask them to make a personal investment in the problem, which greatly enhances the chances that you can create a workable solution together.

All three of the dental professionals in the previous examples knew they had problems and invited the young patients to help them solve those problems. Billy and the dental hygienist agreed on a two-minute "wiggle" period and then a five- minute "be still" period. They alternated periods until the cleaning was completed. Enrique decided to make a better effort at compliance with instructions when he realized his behavior was creating a problem for the dentist. Joanna agreed to abide by quickly constructed red-light and green-light signs for talking and not talking. Her dentist made sure there were enough green-light times so Joanna respected the red-light times.

Are you having a problem with a young patient? Why not invite him or her to join you in the solution-seeking process with, *"I'd like you to help me solve my problem?"*

Follow your words by allowing the child a few minutes to become calm. The brain will slowly shift into higher cortical thinking and frontal lobe activation. When the child has made this transition, the dental practitioner can then use verbal strategies and signature phrases found throughout the Dental Talk book to achieve behavior management goals.

Chapter 6

ODDS AND ENDS

"I don't like what I'm seeing" is designed to send a clear signal to the child - the message that there is something not appropriate about his or her current behavior. The expectation is that the child will pick up on the verbal cue, stop doing whatever he is doing, and choose the desired behavior.

This same phrase and others like it can be used as a different type of signal, one that prompts the adult to engage in a round of inner exploration. "I don't like seeing that behavior" or "I don't like that behavior" or "I'm seeing way too much of that" can serve as a caution to you. It's an indication that you're choosing to see children in a negative light. When you hear yourself saying something like this, stop. Take a moment to redirect your thinking.

Often, we define children by their actions. Many dental practitioners who work with youngsters on a regular basis see particular behaviors and immediately label the child as a troublemaker, whiner, complainer, or reluctant patient. It's important to note that how a practitioner labels children and perceives a given situation strongly affects the outcome of the treatment process.

Remind yourself that each of us sees things differently through the filters of our beliefs, values, ideas, attitudes, and total life experiences. We then interpret what we see in our own unique way. When we look at a behavior, we project onto it whatever it is we have within us. Some see child X as a troublemaker, others see the same child as a potential leader. How we perceive an event or a behavior tells more about us than it does about who or what we saw. It tells about our beliefs, attitudes, and values. Our perception reveals what we have been projecting outward.

Perception is a choice. It is flexible and under our control. Thus, how the dental practitioner sees children is not fixed. It is possible to see children as troublemakers or as crying out for help. It is possible to see them as refusing to sit still and as non-compliant or as having a three-minute attention span and needing a wiggle break. It is possible to see them as whiners or as fearful and needing information to be more comfortable with the process. The dental practitioner's perception will affect what he or she says and does next.

To be of help to these children we must see beyond their act to their essence. Troublemakers are just doing their troublemaking act. Whiners are doing their whiner act. Resistant children are simply doing their resistance act. But that is not the essence of their real selves. It's not the truth about them. It's just their act in the present moment.

"I don't like what I'm seeing" is Dental Talk that can serve as a signal that you have lost sight of this child's real worth. Whether you catch yourself saying it aloud or silently, hear it as a sign that it's time to question your perception. Ask yourself, How am I seeing this? How else could I see it? What else could I be seeing here? How can I see this differently?

"**Check yourself** to see if your hands are out of the way."

"Here's a mirror. **Check yourself** and let me know what you think."

"**Check yourself** to see if you're relaxed enough for me to begin."

"*Check yourself*" is a quick piece of Dental Talk that is useful and adaptable with children of any age. It can be used with young children as a reminder about noise in the waiting room. "I'm having trouble hearing on the telephone. *Please check yourself* to see if you're using your indoor voice." It can be used with ten-year-olds to help them move into a comfortable position. "*Please check yourself* to see if you're in a position that you can maintain for a while." You can use it with teens to encourage an attitude adjustment. "I'm going to be making an impression of your teeth now.

Before I begin, *I'd like you to check yourself* to see if you're mentally ready"

When you add, *"Check yourself,"* to your Dental Talk you send a positive message to your young patients. You tell them by your language and your actions that it is their job to check on themselves, not yours. You move away from ordering and commanding and toward giving children the opportunity to take responsibility for their own actions.

"Make
a picture in your
mind."

One element significantly related to achievement is the ability to visualize desired behaviors and outcomes. Chances are that if you're not able to see yourself behaving a certain way, you will not be able to behave that way. For instance, if you cannot see yourself using the type of language we suggest in this book, you may not use it often or skillfully. Likewise, if a child cannot see herself using her retainer every night, she probably won't do it.

To increase the chances that children will brush regularly, floss, use their retainer at night, or remember their mouth guard for Tae Kwon Do, use the technique of positive picturing. Young children can make a picture in their minds of brushing the tops and the bottoms. Help the martial arts enthusiast to picture packing the mouth guard in his Tae Kwon Do bag, sticking it in his mouth when he gets to the arena, and being hit in the mouth, with the guard serving as protection.

"Make a picture in your mind" helps clarify your expectations for children. It is especially helpful for children whose preferred style of accessing information is visual rather than verbal. Use this language technique to specify the behaviors and levels of performance you want.

"John, while you're holding onto the floss I want you to *make a picture in your mind.* See yourself standing in front of the bathroom mirror at night. Can you see that? Just use your imagination. Notice how you grab the floss with two hands, using pressure to push it down between two teeth. Feel it hit your gums and notice how you slide it back and forth before you pull it out. Now go on to the next tooth and repeat the process. Keep going as you do all the teeth in the bottom of your jaw. Notice how good it feels to have all the food particles out from between your teeth. Now do the top row. Watch as you take each pair of teeth in turn and floss between them. Now look in the mirror and smile. Notice how bright your teeth look and how fresh they taste. Notice how good it feels to have taken care of your flossing responsibility. Now watch as you put the floss container back in the cabinet so it will be where you need it next time."

When you ask a child to make a picture in his mind, you engage his right brain. This is the part of the brain that thinks holistically and is responsible for imagination and intuition. Since most school instruction involves the logical, linear, left brain, positive picturing helps create a balance. When you help a child involve the whole brain, learning increases and success multiplies.

Does picturing the process of flossing insure

that it will be done regularly? Will it guarantee that the mouth guard is worn during sparring? Will it mean that retainers will always be used? Of course not. It will, however, increase your chances of getting the behavior you want more of the time.

"Act your age."

Terrell, age ten, complained of neck pains throughout the session. He had to go to the bathroom twice. He fidgeted in the dental chair and crumpled up his bib. An exasperated dental hygienist, her patience worn thin, finally asked him, "Terrell, why don't you act your age?"

Actually, Terrell was acting his age. Developmental characteristics of school-age children under stress include complaining of pain, wiggling, and asking to use the bathroom. Terrell is being chastised for being a typical stressed-out ten-year-old.

It's not uncommon for dental practitioners to want children to act like little adults. Forget it. It isn't going to happen. Children are not little adults. They are children and will exhibit normal characteristics of children their age. Although all young patients are individuals, their behavior will often fit into a predictable framework that is age appropriate.

Dental practitioners who understand human

growth and the predictable behavioral characteristics of children are less likely to view age-appropriate behavior as misbehavior. When your staff understands the developmental reasons behind the forgetfulness of seven-year-olds or the moodiness of preadolescents, they will be more accepting of children and less likely to think or say, "Act your age." It will then be possible for them to approach children's behaviors from a calm and understanding stance. They will feel less provoked and stressed and more able to respond with warmth and acceptance.

If you want to work successfully with children, it's essential that you develop a clear understanding of the stages of child development. For more information on this topic, go to **www.dentaltalk.net** to download our special report, "Children: Ages and Stages."

"Act your age" is not instructional Dental Talk. It does nothing to teach the child the behavior you want. If you want her to manifest certain behaviors and reduce or eliminate others, you must first accept her where she is in the present moment, while suggesting and encouraging specific behavioral alternatives.

Instead of helping children understand what behaviors are expected, "Act your age" communicates disrespect, misunderstanding, and impatience. If you wish to make your language congruent with a desire to build a positive long-term relationship with a child, eliminate "Act your age" from your Dental Talk.

"NOW THAT WE HAVE THE DENTAL INSURANCE, IT WAS PRACTICALLY MY <u>DUTY</u> TO HAVE A CAVITY."

A B O U T   T H E   A U T H O R S

Portraits by Gregg

Thomas B. Haller,
MDiv, LMSW, DST

Thomas Haller currently works in private practice at Shinedling, Shinedling, and Haller, P.C., in Bay City, Michigan, as a child, adolescent, and couples therapist; an individual psychotherapist; and a chronic pain counselor. He is a certified EEG biofeedback technician, an AASECT Certified Diplomate Sex

Therapist, and a certified sports counselor. Thomas has extensive training in psychotherapy with children and couples from the University of Michigan, where he received his Master of Social Work degree. He is also an ordained Lutheran minister with a Master of Divinity degree from Concordia Theological Seminary.

Thomas is a widely sought-after national and international presenter in the areas of parenting, interpersonal relationships, and chronic pain. He is also the founder and director of Healing Minds Institute, a center devoted to teaching others how to enhance their health of their mind, body, and spirit. Thomas conducts workshops and seminars for churches, school districts, parent groups, and counseling agencies. He is also a regular lecturer at universities across the country.

Contact information:

Thomas Haller
Shinedling, Shinedling, and Haller, P.C.
2355 1/2 Delta Rd.
Bay City, MI 48706
Telephone: (989) 667-5654
Fax: (989) 667-5330
E-mail: thomas@thomashaller.com
Website: http://www.thomashaller.com

Portraits by Gregg

Chick Moorman

Chick Moorman is the director of the Institute for Personal Power, a consulting firm dedicated to providing high-quality professional development activities for educators, parents, and health-care professionals.

He is a former classroom teacher with over 40 years of experience in the field of education. His mission is to help people experience a greater sense of personal power in their lives so they can in turn empower others.

Chick conducts full-day workshops and seminars for school districts and parent groups. He also delivers keynote addresses for local, state, and national conferences.

Contact information:

Chick Moorman
P.O. Box 547
Merrill, MI 48637
Telephone: (877) 360-1477
Fax: (989) 643-5156
E-mail: ipp57@aol.com
Website: http://www.chickmoorman.com

OTHER BOOKS AND PRODUCTS

THE 10 COMMITMENTS: *Parenting with Purpose,* by Chick Moorman and Thomas Haller ($20.00)

COUPLE TALK: *How to Talk Your Way to a Great Relationship,* by Chick Moorman and Thomas Haller ($25.00)

SPIRIT WHISPERERS: *Teachers Who Nourish a Child's Spirit,* by Chick Moorman ($25.00)

PARENT TALK: *How to Talk to Your Children in Language That Builds Self-Esteem and Encourages Responsibility,* by Chick Moorman ($13.00)

TEACHER TALK: *What It Really Means,* by Chick Moorman and Nancy Weber ($13.00)

WHERE THE HEART IS: *Stories of Home and Family,* by Chick Moorman ($15.00)

TALK SENSE TO YOURSELF: *The Language of Personal Power,* by Chick Moorman ($13.00)

OUR CLASSROOM: *We Can Learn Together,* by Chick Moorman and Dee Dishon ($20.00)

THE LANGUAGE OF RESPONSE-ABLE PARENT-ING, audiocassette series featuring Chick Moorman ($39.95)

PARENT TALK FOCUS CARDS, by Chick Moorman ($10.00)

THE PARENT TALK SYSTEM: *The Language of Response-Able Parenting, Facilitator's Manual,* by Chick Moorman, Sarah Knapp, and Judith Minton ($300.00)

Order from Personal Power Press

Order toll-free: 1-877-360-1477
Fax (24 hours):   1-989-643-5156
Email: ipp57@aol.com
Mail: **Personal Power Press, P.O. Box 547, Merrill, MI 48637**

Product #	Qty.	Description	Price Each	Total

Subtotal	
Tax MI residents 6%	
Shipping and handling (see chart below)	
TOTAL	

turn page to complete order form

Please add the following shipping & handling charges:
$1-$15.00 . . . .$3.75
$15.01-$30.00 . . . . . .$4.75
$30.01-$50.00 . . . . . .$5.75
$50.01 and up 10% of total order
Canada: 20% of total order. U.S. funds only, please.

Method of Payment

☐ American Express ☐ Discover ☐ VISA
☐ MasterCard ☐ Check/Money Order (payable in U.S. funds)

Card # _ _ _ _ - _ _ _ _ - _ _ _ _ - _ _ _ _

Expiration Date: _____

Daytime Phone: (_____) _____

Signature: _____

Ship To:

Name: _____

Address: _____

City: _____

State: _____ Zip: _____

Email: _____

Daytime Phone: (____) _____

Nighttime Phone: (____) _____

School Purchase Orders readily accepted.

Mail to: **PERSONAL POWER PRESS, INC.,**
P.O. Box 547, Merrill, MI 48637
Phone: (877) 360-1477 - Fax: (989) 643-5156 -
Email: IPP57@aol.com
Web Site: www.chickmoorman.com & www.thomashaller.com

OUR VISION: HEALING ACRES

A portion of the proceeds from *Dental Talk: How to Manage Children's Behavior with Effective Verbal Skills* will be used to support an equine retirement ranch. One dollar from each book sold will go toward the maintenance of Healing Acres Equine Retirement Ranch.

The goal of Healing Acres Ranch is to provide a peaceful and caring environment for aged horses that have devoted many years of service. It will include a low-stress atmosphere, room to exercise and graze freely, adequate shelter, and preventive and attentive health care for all horses.

Other services planned for Healing Acres Ranch, Inc. include therapeutic riding for persons with disabilities and equine-assisted psychotherapy.

If you wish to make a donation beyond the purchase of this book, please visit our website: **www.healingacres.com**

Thank you for helping us support this vision.